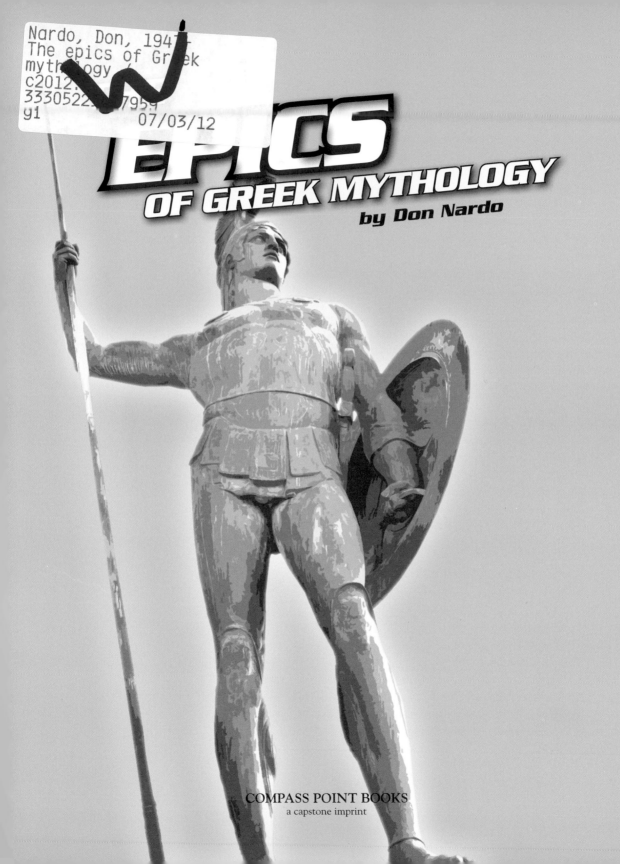

EPICS
OF GREEK MYTHOLOGY
by Don Nardo

COMPASS POINT BOOKS
a capstone imprint

Compass Point Books
151 Good Counsel Drive
P.O. Box 669
Mankato, MN 56002-0669

Editors: Sarah Eason and Geoff Barker
Designers: Paul Myerscough and Simon Borrough
Media Researcher: Susannah Jayes
Content Consultant: Michael Vickers, DLitt., Professor of Archaeology, University of Oxford
Production Specialist: Laura Manthe

Image Credits
Alamy: A F Archive 52–53, Interfoto 14, 49, Ivy Close Images 35, Leslie Garland Picture Library
56, Mary Evans Picture Library 20–21, 38, 45, Robert Harding Picture Library Ltd 54, A. T. Willett
56–57; **Bridgeman:** Photo © Christie's Images 16, Private Collection / The Stapleton Collection 32,
Villa Valmarana ai Nani, Vicenza, Italy/Alinari 4–5; **Corbis:** The Art Archive 12–13; **Geoff Ward:**
cover (front), 8–9, 25, 28–29, 30–31, 42, 50–51; **Istock:** Thinkstock chapter 1 bgd, Duncan Walker
55; **Shutterstock:** Algol 59 (bottom), Vartanov Anatoly 17, Anton Balazh 22, EcoPrint 18–19,
eugeneharnam 52 (back), 64, Imagix 58 (bottom), 59 (top left), Kamira 36, Panos Karapanagiotis 1,
11, Georgy Markov 6, Paul B. Moore 23, NesaCera 34, 39, Michael Onisiforou cover (bottom bgd), Nick
Pavlakis 19 (right), Petrafler 59 (top right), Andrejs Pidjass 40–41, Noel Powell, Schaumburg 26–27,
Raulin 2–3, chapter 2 bgd, 60–61, Rikitiki 58 (top), Fesus Robert 46–47.

Library of Congress Cataloging-in-Publication Data
Nardo, Don, 1947-
  The epics of Greek mythology / by Don Nardo.
      p. cm.—(Ancient Greek mythology)
  Includes bibliographical references and index.
  ISBN 978-0-7565-4482-9 (library binding)
  1. Homer—Influence—Juvenile literature. 2. Homer. Iliad—Juvenile literature. 3. Homer. Odyssey
—Juvenile literature. 4. Epic poetry, Greek—Stories, plots, etc.—Juvenile literature. 5. Epic poetry,
Greek—History and criticism—Juvenile literature. 6. Mythology, Greek, in literature—Juvenile
literature. 7. Civilization, Western—Greek influences—Juvenile literature. I. Title.
  PA4037.N365 2012
  883'.01—dc22   2011015244
Visit Compass Point Books on the Internet at *www.capstonepub.com*

Printed in the United States of America in Stevens Point, Wisconsin.
082011   006341R

TABLE OF CONTENTS

Chapter 1

THE DAWN OF WESTERN LITERATURE

In 1757 artist Giovanni Battista Tiepolo used the *Iliad* as his inspiration to paint the nymph Thetis consoling her son Achilles.

Western culture spread across the world in early modern times. The European-based culture, which thrives in the United States, Canada, Mexico, Australia, and New Zealand, along with Europe itself, traces its roots back to ancient Greece. Western civilization was quite literally established by the ancient Greeks. They invented politics, democracy, and the theater. They also introduced the first philosophical and scientific concepts and methods. In addition, the Greeks gave Western society its alphabet, architectural styles that are still used for all manner of public buildings, and the Olympic Games.

As if all that were not enough, the ancient Greeks also ignited the dawn of Western literature. The Greeks invented nearly all of the literary forms and disciplines known today, including drama, historical writing, and the novel. Logic would dictate that these and other kinds of literature begin with simple, primitive forms. Over time they would slowly grow more complex and sophisticated. This was not the case, however. Just the opposite occurred. The first two examples of Western literature were nothing short of masterpieces. Grand, complex, and moving, they came to be seen by both the ancient and modern worlds as the height of literary creation.

The Poet

The two works are the epic poems the *Iliad* and *Odyssey*. The first deals with a series of episodes in the last year of the Trojan War. In that famous mythical conflict, an alliance of Greek kings besieged Troy, a prosperous trading city in Asia Minor (what is now Turkey). The second epic, the *Odyssey*, traces the adventures of one of those Greek kings, Odysseus, after Troy's fall.

The first versions of the two works likely appeared sometime in the the 800s BC. Initially they were passed on orally by traveling storytellers called bards. They recited them and other mythical tales from memory, adding a few new details or improving existing lines and phrases. In this way, the poems grew longer and more polished over time.

One of the bards eventually gained primary credit for the *Iliad* and *Odyssey*. His name was Homer. No one knows where and when he was born. The Greek island of Chios, off Asia Minor's western coast, is a strong candidate for where. As for when, the mid-700s BC seems likely. And nothing is definitely known about his life.

What seems more certain is that Homer brought the two epics to their final and greatest forms. Exactly how he did this is unknown. It does appear that the art of writing developed in Greece during his lifetime. It may be that he dictated the epics to a scribe a little at a time. That would have allowed him to add more complex detail than was normally done when reciting the works.

Homer, the greatest name in epic poetry, is usually portrayed as a blind man.

Also, once committed to paper, the poems would stop
evolving. They would have become in a sense frozen
in their now familiar form.

However he did it, Homer made the *Iliad* and *Odyssey* his
own. He gained a standing as a writer and myth-teller that
was second to none. His reputation became so great that
for the rest of ancient times people across the known world
referred to him, with a touch of awe, as "the Poet."

Huge Influence

The *Iliad* and *Odyssey* did much more than ensure that Homer
would be fondly remembered, however. These works laid
the groundwork for the huge burst of literary activity the
Greeks produced in the centuries that followed. Moreover, the
two epics had an enormous influence on Greek culture and
thought. As classical scholar Michael Grant has pointed out,
these works exerted a profound civilizing influence on the
Greeks. The epics, he said:

> formed the foundation of their literary, artistic, moral,
> social, educational, and political attitudes. For a long
> time no histories of early times seemed at all necessary,
> since the Iliad and Odyssey fulfilled every requirement.
> They attracted universal esteem and reverence, too, as
> sources of general and practical wisdom, as arguments
> for heroic yet human nobility and dignity, as incentives
> to vigorous (often warlike) manly action, and as mines
> of endless quotations and commentaries, the common
> property of Greeks everywhere.

Homer's epics also had a tremendous effect on the development of classical Greek religion and mythology. This is because the works contain thousands of references to the Greek gods. Among them are descriptions of the deities' physical appearances, personalities, powers, and strengths and weaknesses. As German scholar Walter Otto put it, each god described by Homer "possesses its special character, clearly defined in all its traits. [The] listener has a vivid idea of the being and essence of every god. Whenever [Homer] introduces a god, he characterizes him in a few strokes."

Just as important, Homer depicted the superhuman beings, along with mythical monsters, as interacting with humans. That interaction included various forms of worship. Thus, in addition to their many other qualities, the *Iliad* and *Odyssey* became manuals for understanding and worshipping the gods.

Zeus and other gods played their part in shaping the events of the *Iliad* and *Odyssey*.

That practical religious function of Homer's epics was no longer relevant after the Greek religion ceased to exist at the close of ancient times, in the 400s and 500s AD. The epics themselves survived, however. In early modern times they were translated into many languages, partially memorized by schoolchildren, and studied in colleges. They also came to be endlessly read, recited, and quoted by writers, national leaders, and ordinary folk. "Soldiers have gone into battle with lines from Homer on their lips," historian Ernle Bradford wrote. "Statesmen have quoted [the epics] in grave debates and conferences, and poets have tried (vainly) over the centuries to rival [their] story-telling power."

The power to keep an audience entertained for hours remains one of the chief qualities of the *Iliad* and *Odyssey* today. In part that is because these works remain rich sources of information about mythological characters and deeds. They are chock-full of action, adventure, valiant heroes, superhuman beings both good and evil, and terrifying monsters. In these and other ways, they are the direct predecessors of modern epic fantasies such as the *Lord of the Rings* trilogy and the *Star Wars* series. Homer's epics have thrilled and inspired audiences for nearly 3,000 years. There seems little doubt that they will continue to do so for many centuries to come.

Chapter 2

THE ILIAD:
A Warrior Refuses to Fight

Homer's immortal *Iliad* is the tale of a mighty warrior who, for reasons he viewed as just, decided to stop fighting. The warrior was a Greek named Achilles. His refusal to leave his tent and lead his fellow Greeks in battle occurred in the 10th year of the legendary Trojan War. His decision had serious consequences. But before they can be revealed, we must consider how he arrived at that fateful moment.

The great war against Troy, like so many other conflicts in history, came about because someone powerful felt slighted. One day Zeus and several other gods were enjoying themselves at a lavish party in one of their palaces atop Mount Olympus. They were celebrating the wedding of a sea nymph named Thetis. By chance, the minor goddess happened to be the mother of the formidable warrior Achilles.

Name:
Achilles

Roman name:
Achilles

Family:
son of sea nymph Thetis and Peleus, king of the Myrmidons

Known for:
being skilled in battle, Greece's finest fighter

Famous myth:
killed Trojan hero Hector in the Trojan War, as described in Homer's *Iliad*

The great Greek warrior Achilles is known for his single weak spot, his heel.

But someone had forgotten to invite another minor goddess—Eris. The deity of discord, she was well known for her nasty temper. So when the feast started without her, she did what she did best—she stirred up trouble. Eris wrote the words "for the most beautiful goddess" on a golden apple, then tossed it into the midst of the party. Just as she had anticipated, every goddess in attendance assumed the apple was meant for her. Three of the proud deities—Hera, Athena, and Aphrodite—hurried to Zeus. They implored him to choose which of them was indeed the most attractive and worthy of the golden apple. But Zeus was too smart to get involved. He knew that after choosing a winner he would have to deal with the disappointment and anger of the other two goddesses.

The Judgment of Paris

Zeus offered the three anxious deities an alternative plan. They should travel to Mount Ida, near the city of Troy, on the far side of the Aegean Sea. A Trojan prince named Paris had recently become renowned as a good judge of beauty, Zeus said. They should find Paris and ask him which goddess was the fairest.

Hera, Athena, and Aphrodite flew at top speed to Mount Ida and sought out Paris. The young man was surprised to find himself surrounded by three divinities, who towered over him. He was also quite bewildered when they demanded that he hold a beauty contest with himself as the judge.

Paris' hard decision was depicted in a work of art by the 17th century painter Francesco Rosa.

12

Just before the contest began, each goddess secretly approached the youth and offered him a bribe. Hera said she would make him king of the known world. Athena offered to make him the chief hero in a war between the Greeks and Trojans. Aphrodite claimed she would cause the most gorgeous of all mortal women to fall madly in love with him. The result of the competition, which became known as the "Judgment of Paris," was that Paris chose Aphrodite as victor.

The goddess of love was so thrilled at winning the golden apple that she immediately proceeded to keep the promise she'd made to Paris. The identity of the most attractive human woman was no mystery. Everyone knew she was Helen, queen of the Greek kingdom of Sparta. The fact that she had a husband, King Menelaus, seemed to be no obstacle to Aphrodite. The goddess took Paris to Sparta and made arrangements for him to be welcomed as a guest in the palace. No sooner had this occurred than Menelaus left Sparta on royal business. Just as quickly, Paris and Helen fell deeply in love, and he persuaded her to go back to Troy with him.

Paris left his wife Oenone for the beautiful queen Helen of Sparta (left). This action triggered the Trojan War.

Preparing for the Expedition

When Menelaus returned home, he was enraged that Prince Paris had stolen his wife. The Spartan ruler rushed to Mycenae, northeast of Sparta, where his brother, Agamemnon, was king. Menelaus asked Agamemnon to raise troops from cities and kingdoms all across Greece. The main goal was to get Helen back. But if they could loot Troy and divide the spoils in the process, all the better.

Name:
Odysseus

Roman name:
Ulysses

Family:
son of Laertes and Anticleia; husband of Penelope; father of Telemachus

Known for:
skill with sword, quick mind

Famous myth:
20-year journey home, described in the epic *Odyssey*

Most of the Greek kings and heroes who were asked to join the great expedition against Troy accepted right away. One of the few who was not very eager to go was Thetis' son Achilles, the finest soldier in Greece. Years before, when he was a baby, she had lowered his body into the River Styx, the waterway running along the edge of the Underworld. As a result, his skin resisted all wounds. The single exception was the heel she'd held while dipping him into the magical waters. Thetis did not want Achilles to go to Troy because she had once heard a divine prophecy. It had claimed that if there were a war between the Greeks and Trojans, her son would die in the conflict. For that reason, Thetis sent Achilles to live with his rich uncle, who had him wear women's clothes as a disguise.

Achilles was unable to escape detection for long, however. Odysseus, king of the Greek island kingdom of Ithaca, who was known for his wisdom, found him. The wily Odysseus donned his own disguise— that of a traveling salesman—and went to Achilles' uncle's large mansion. The supposed peddler showed off some perfumes, ribbons, makeup, and other items to the women of the house. But he also offered a fine new sword. While the women were admiring the items, Odysseus noticed that one of them passed over all but the sword, which "she" eagerly swung back and forth. Realizing he had found Achilles, the Ithacan king yanked off the other man's disguise. Odysseus then persuaded the great warrior to join the coming expedition.

The allied Greek forces gathered in Aulis, on Greece's eastern coast. There the expedition's leaders had amassed a thousand warships. (For that reason, people in later ages would say that Helen had "the face that launched a thousand ships.") Besides Odysseus and Achilles, the leaders included Helen's husband, Menelaus, and his brother, Agamemnon, the overall commander. Also prominent among the Greeks were Ajax, a giant of a man famous for his strength and courage, and Achilles' best friend, Patroclus.

A few days later, the enormous armada reached the sandy coastline near Troy. The Greeks beached their vessels and made camp near a wide, windy plain that stretched in front of the city. Then Agamemnon, Achilles, and the others took the time to size up their opponents. It was clear that victory would not be easy. Troy's stone defensive walls were solid and high. Also, it was well known that the city's king, Priam, had many fine warriors. The most formidable among them was his son, Hector. Rumor had it that he might even be a match for Achilles.

> Determined to defeat their enemies, the Greeks sailed to Troy.

The Greeks' concern that taking the city would be difficult proved well founded. The siege dragged on for more than nine years, and many brave fighters died on both sides. Yet in all that time neither side was able to gain a major advantage.

The Quarrel over the Women

In the war's 10th year an unexpected incident occurred. A Trojan priest of Apollo, god of prophecy and healing, appeared in the Greek camp. The Greek supreme commander, Agamemnon, was holding his daughter, Chryseis, the Trojan said. If Agamemnon would let the girl go, the priest would give the Greeks a large amount of silver and gold. Several of the foremost Greeks urged their leader to agree to the deal. But Agamemnon refused. Rebuffed, the furious priest went to his altar and prayed for Apollo to punish the Greeks until they freed Chryseis. The god heard the prayer and, according to Homer:

> came down in a fury from the heights of Olympus with his bow and covered quiver on his back. [He] sat down opposite the [Greek] ships and shot an arrow, with a dreadful twang from his silver bow. He attacked the mules first and [then] he aimed his sharp arrows at the men, and struck again and again. Day and night, innumerable [funeral] fires consumed the dead. For nine days the god's arrows rained on the camp.

Name:
Hector

Roman name:
Hector

Family:
son of King Priam of Troy and Hecuba; one of 50 offspring

Known for:
being skilled in battle, Troy's finest fighter

Famous myth:
key role as fighter in Trojan War, described in Homer's *Iliad*; known for his fatal duel with Achilles

The helmets of the Greek soldiers were protective and fearsome.

Finally Achilles convened a meeting of the Greek leaders. Supported by the others, he demanded that Agamemnon release Chryseis so that Apollo would stop his attacks. Agamemnon reluctantly agreed. As soon as he let Chryseis go, Apollo halted his onslaught against the Greek camp. However, Agamemnon decided to retaliate against Achilles for forcing him to release his captive. The supreme commander seized one of Achilles' own favorite captives, a girl named Briseis.

Achilles was outraged over the loss of young Briseis. In a huff, he announced that he was retiring to his tent. He and his men would no longer fight for Agamemnon, he said. This marked a major change in the Greeks' fortunes of war. Achilles was their greatest warrior, and if he refused to lead them in battle, they were at a distinct disadvantage. Deep concern over what had happened spread rapidly through the Greek camp.

Agamemnon's Dream

The angry Achilles prayed to his mother, the sea goddess Thetis, and she heard his words. As Homer described it, she "rose swiftly from the gray water like a mist," and sat beside her son. She asked why he was so distressed, and he told her about his quarrel with Agamemnon. Then he asked her to speak with Zeus on his behalf. "Go to Olympus," he implored, "and if anything you have ever done or said has warmed the heart of Zeus, remind him of it as you pray to him."

Thetis did as her son had requested. She sped to snow-capped Olympus and found the all-seeing Zeus sitting by himself on one of its many peaks. "Father Zeus!" she said.

If ever I have served you well among the gods, by word or deed, grant me this wish and show your favor to my son! He is already singled out for early death, and now Agamemnon, King of Men, has [insulted] him. He has stolen his prize and kept her for himself. Avenge my son, Olympian Judge, and let the Trojans have the upper hand till the Greeks pay him due respect and make him full amends."

Zeus made no reply to this. He sat in silence for a long time, with Thetis clinging to his knees.

Zeus did not like taking sides in the war, but in time he decided to do as Thetis had asked. The master of the thunderbolt knew that the Greeks counted on Achilles' strength and valor in battle. So Zeus sent Agamemnon a false dream. In it the supreme commander was urged to attack Troy in full force even though Achilles was not in the ranks.

After waking up, Agamemnon decided to heed the advice he had received in the dream. He ordered the assault. Just before the battle began, however, Hector advised his brother Paris to make an offer of single combat to King Menelaus. It was their rivalry over Helen, after all, that had ignited the war in the first place. Paris agreed with Hector and made the offer to Menelaus, who accepted.

King Menelaus grabbed Paris' helmet during their famous fight. The king was winning, but Aphrodite saved Paris.

The two men fought each other before Troy's towering walls as the soldiers of the two armies watched. Soon it became clear that Paris was losing the duel. As Homer told it, Menelaus "seized him by the horse-hair crest [on his helmet] and began to drag him into the Greek lines." Fortunately for Paris, at that moment his personal protector, Aphrodite, leapt into the fray. "Hiding Paris in a dense mist, she whisked him off [and] put him down in his own perfumed fragrant bedroom."

Watching the battle from above, Aphrodite took pity on Paris and came to his rescue.

Name:
Menelaus

Roman name:
Menelaus

Family:
husband of Helen, brother of Agamemnon

Known for:
bravery in battle, leader of Greek army

Famous myth:
Homer's *Iliad* describes how he loses his wife to Paris and fights a duel

Not long after the indecisive end of the fight between Paris and Menelaus, the full armies finally clashed. The valiant warriors exchanged blows, and some died holding their blood stained shields. Also, various gods, supporting one side or the other, could be seen, their enormous frames standing out clearly in the midst of the conflict. Eventually the great Hector led the Trojans in a mighty assault that drove the Greeks backward almost to their camp.

The Battle for the Beaches

The Greeks now found themselves in a dangerous situation. One of their leaders, Nestor of Pylos, told Agamemnon that a "calamity is certainly upon us!" The Trojans had breached a defensive wall the Greeks had earlier erected near the beaches, Nestor pointed out. As a result, "our men are committed to a long and desperate fight beside the gallant ships!"

Apollo infused Hector with agility and speed, saving him from defeat.

Name:
Apollo

Roman name:
Apollo

Group:
Olympian

Family:
son of Zeus and Leto, brother of Artemis

Responsibility:
poetry, healing, music, archery

Symbol:
laurel tree

As the bloody battle raged, the giant Greek warrior Ajax caught sight of Hector eagerly leading the Trojans forward. Ajax picked up a rock so big that his own men were amazed. He hurled it at Hector, striking him "on the chest just below the neck, over the rim of his shield, making him spin and travel around like a top. Thus Hector in his gallantry was brought down into the dust."

Fortunately for Hector, Apollo saw what had happened. The god hurried to the fallen man and swiftly healed him, making him even stronger and more energetic than before. As Homer described it, Apollo:

> breathed power into the Trojan commander, who now ran off on nimble feet with lightened limbs. He was like a stallion who breaks his halter [and] gallops off across the fields in triumph . . . skimming the ground with his feet.

Like a Savage Lion

After Hector had recovered from the wounds he'd received at Ajax's hands, Homer wrote, he attacked the Greeks like a force of nature:

> At last Hector, aflame from head to foot, burst into [the enemy's] midst. Picture a wave raised by a gale and sweeping forward under the scudding clouds. It breaks on a gallant ship. [The] angry wind booms in her sail, and the crew, saved from destruction by a hair's breadth, are left trembling and aghast. This is how Hector fell upon the Greeks, striking panic into their hearts. And they stampeded, as cattle do when a savage lion finds them grazing in their hundreds.

Name:
Patroclus

Roman name:
Patroclus

Family:
son of Menoetius

Known for:
being a daring, if somewhat
foolhardy, warrior

Famous myth:
wears the armor of
his best friend Achilles
to try to trick the
Trojans in war

With Hector revived, the Trojans hammered the Greeks, sending a wave of fear through their ranks. Brave Patroclus looked out on the seeming rout of his countrymen and sighed loudly. He knew that if his good friend Achilles left his tent and led the Greeks once more, they might turn the impending defeat into a victory. Running to Achilles' tent, he begged the other man to re-enter the fray. "What will future generations have to thank you for if you will not help the Greeks in their direst need?" Patroclus asked. But Achilles still said no. Patroclus then declared that if his friend would not fight,

> at least allow me to take the field [so that] I might yet bring
> salvation to the Greeks. And lend me your own armor to put
> on my shoulders so that the Trojans may take me for you
> and break off the battle, which would give our weary troops
> time to recuperate [rest].

Although Achilles would not fight, he agreed to lend his armor to Patroclus, who, wearing it, entered the battle. Thinking that mighty Achilles had rejoined their ranks, the Greeks rallied. The Trojans, fearing Achilles' wrath, fell back onto the plain and retreated toward the city. Soon, however, the daring but foolhardy Patroclus encountered Hector himself. The two fought and Patroclus fell dead in the dirt. Hector stripped Achilles' armor off the man, and several Greeks carried Patroclus' body back to their camp.

Two Great Champions Clash

When the news of Patroclus' death reached Achilles, both he and the course of the war instantly changed. His divine mother, Thetis, had Hephaestus, god of the forge, make new armor for her son. Achilles swore he would neither eat nor sleep until he'd avenged his slain friend. Then he led the Greeks in a fierce offensive against the Trojans. Many gods once more took sides and entered the conflict.

Patroclus borrowed Achilles' armor to deceive the Trojan troops.

The Gods Go to War

As Achilles re-entered the fight, so too did many of the gods, who created a terrible commotion. According to Homer:

Up on high the Father of men and gods thundered ominously, and down below Poseidon caused the wide world and the lofty mountain-tops to quake. Every spur and crest of [Mount] Ida … was shaken. The Trojan city and the ships of the Greeks trembled. And in the Underworld, Hades, King of the Dead, took fright and leapt with a cry from his throne. He was afraid that Poseidon and his earthquakes might split open the ground above his head and expose to mortal and immortal eyes the hateful chambers of decay that fill the gods themselves with horror. Such was the turmoil as the battle of the gods began.

The Trojans were unable to resist the reawakened Greeks and gods. Troy's gates opened to receive its fleeing troops, then closed before the Greeks could follow them in. Hector alone remained outside to face the fuming Achilles. The greatest warrior that Greece had and Troy's finest fighter rushed at each other. In Homer's words:

> Hector charged, brandishing his sharp sword [and] Achilles sprang to meet him, inflamed with savage passion. He kept his front covered with his decorated shield. His glittering helmet with its four plates swayed as he moved his head [and] the sharp point shimmered on the spear he balanced in his right hand, intent on killing Hector.

With a crash of metal on metal, the two champions collided, and loud cheers rang out from the watching armies. As Achilles and Hector came to death grips, each searched for some opening on the other's body. Achilles, according to Homer, saw one "at the gullet where the collar bones lead over from the shoulders to the neck." Hector leapt at him, and as he did so:

> Achilles drove at this spot with his lance and the point went right through the tender flesh of Hector's neck. [Seconds later] Hector came down in the dust and the great Achilles triumphed over him. [The onset of] death cut Hector short and his disembodied soul took wing for the House of Hades.

Beware of Greeks Bearing Gifts

The triumphant Achilles now raised a victory shout, which his countrymen loudly echoed. Finishing his revenge, he tore off Hector's armor and tied the dead body to the back of his chariot. Then he dragged the bloody corpse around Troy's high walls. It took many hours for Achilles' fury to subside, but eventually he agreed to give Hector's remains to King Priam, who presided over the slain hero's funeral. There was a funeral, too, on the Greek side for valiant Patroclus.

Odysseus was the architect of the wooden horse, which was used to fool the Trojans.

Achilles was not fated to survive Hector
for long, however. When the fighting
resumed, Prince Paris shot an arrow
that Apollo guided to the single
weak spot on Achilles' body.
It was the heel by which his divine
mother had held him when he was an
infant. Achilles fell dead from the wound. (Ever since,
a person's greatest weakness has been called his
Achilles heel.)

In the weeks that followed, more killing ensued and
many more brave warriors fell on both sides. Finally
the wily Odysseus told Agamemnon that he had a plan
that could bring the Greeks victory. If they built a large
wooden horse, some of them could hide inside. That
might gain them entry into the enemy city.

Odysseus oversaw the horse's construction, after
which he and several companions hid inside.
Leaving it near the beach, the other Greeks
boarded their ships and sailed away. The Trojans
saw the strange object in the distance and
some of them left the city to investigate.
They had just reached it when a Greek named
Sinon appeared. He told them that his
countrymen had left him behind
by accident. The great horse, he
explained, was meant as a gift
for Athena, goddess of war.

Sinon was lying, of course. He was delighted when the Trojans believed him, dragged the horse into the city, and celebrated wildly, thinking they'd won the war. After several hours, the partying ended. Everyone in the city, except for a few guards, fell fast asleep. Sensing that the time was right, Odysseus and his companions climbed out of the horse's hollow belly. They quietly crept through the city, killed the guards, and used a torch to give a signal. Under the cover of darkness, the Greek ships had returned. Agamemnon and his men saw the signal and rushed through Troy's gates, which Odysseus had opened. (The wooden horse had accomplished its deceptive and lethal purpose. In later ages people would remember it in the phrase "Beware of Greeks bearing gifts.")

Odysseus lit a torch to signal the Greeks on ships to come back to Troy and defeat the Trojans.

In this way King Priam's proud city fell to the Greeks, who took Helen back, then looted and burned the place. A few Trojans survived. One was Priam's son Aeneas, who was destined to journey westward to distant Italy. There, his descendants would establish another great city—Rome. With the long war finally over, the Greeks sailed back to their homes—all, that is, except for Odysseus and his men. Fate was about to take them on another epic adventure that Homer would immortalize in his verses.

Chapter 3
THE ODYSSEY:
A Soldier Searches for Home

The 10-year-long siege of Troy by the Greeks had ended with the city's demise. In large part the Greek victory had been made possible by the talents of one of the Greek leaders—Odysseus (whom the Romans called Ulysses), king of Ithaca. He had a sturdy frame, curly, reddish-brown hair, and a full beard. Though skilled with a sword and bow, Odysseus was best known for his cleverness. Indeed, it was he who had conceived of building a huge, hollow wooden horse at the battle of Troy.

Odysseus was a great archer. His skill with the bow is displayed at the end of the *Odyssey*.

-T.H.-
-Robinson-

Odysseus watched Troy burn and prepared for his departure with the 12 ships he'd brought with him 10 years before. He looked forward to sailing back to his island kingdom. With its pleasant, rolling green hills, Ithaca lay on the far side of the Greek mainland. To get there from Troy required crossing the Aegean Sea. Then one sailed southward around the Peloponnesus, the large peninsula making up Greece's lower third.

It was not only Ithaca's physical beauty that Odysseus pictured when thinking about home. He also longed to see his beloved wife, Penelope. There was also their son, Telemachus, who had been a small child when Odysseus had left for Troy. Finally, Odysseus fondly remembered his faithful dog, Argus. Soon, he told himself, he would finally be reunited with these loved ones after being parted from them for so long.

Odysseus Begins Telling His Story

Unfortunately for Odysseus, he was not destined to enjoy that happy homecoming soon. He and his men became the unwitting victims of another man's poor judgment and irreverent acts. While the Greek soldiers were capturing and looting Troy, one of them did a terrible thing. He forced his way into the local temple of Athena, goddess of war and wisdom. Then he brutally raped one of the Trojan king's daughters. She had earlier entered the temple to seek the goddess' protection.

When Athena found out about this sacrilege, she was furious. She persuaded her father, Zeus, leader of the Olympian gods, to punish as many of the Greeks as possible. He whipped up a huge storm. Its high winds and enormous waves battered the Greek ships as they headed homeward from Troy. Most of the vessels and crews managed to survive the tempest in one piece. But some of the men drowned and some of the ships were blown off course. Among the latter were the ships of Odysseus and his men, who became lost and wandered from one strange place to another.

Homer described Odysseus' adventures in considerable detail. But his tale began when the Ithacan king was in the 10th year of his wanderings. At that point Athena went to Ithaca in disguise and met with Odysseus' grown son, Telemachus. She urged him to find out whether his father was still alive. Telemachus journeyed to Sparta and talked with King Menelaus. The king told Telemachus that he'd heard a rumor. It claimed that Odysseus was alive and was being held captive on the island of a nymph named Calypso.

Odysseus' son Telemachus was desperate to see the father he had never met.

Feeling bad for Odysseus, Athena sped to Mount Olympus and spoke with Zeus. At her urgings, the king of the gods sent word to Calypso that she must allow Odysseus to go free. Reluctantly, the nymph gave her captive the materials to construct a small boat. Odysseus built the vessel and sailed away. But Poseidon, lord of the seas, remembered an offense Odysseus had committed against him years before and caused the boat to capsize. Struggling in the churning waves, Odysseus saw land in the distance. With the little strength he had left, he swam to it and dragged himself onto the beach.

The island turned out to be the homeland of a pleasant people who called themselves the Phaeacians. After Odysseus had regained his strength, the Phaeacian ruler gave a feast in his honor. The Greek's hosts asked him about the travels that had led him to their island. He explained that shortly after leaving Troy, he and his men had encountered an awful storm. It had tossed them to and fro until they were completely lost.

With his mastery of the oceans, Poseidon could command the waves to crush a fleet of ships.

Eventually they reached an island inhabited by a people called the Lotus-eaters, who ate only plants. These strange folk offered some of the men an intoxicating herb that caused them to become lazy and to forget about reaching their homes. Odysseus recalled:

> *I had to use force to bring them back to the ships, and they wept on the way, but once on board I dragged them under the benches and left them in irons. I then commanded the rest of my loyal band to embark with all speed on their fast ships, for fear that others of them might eat the lotus and think no more of home.*

Island of the Giants

Continuing his story, Odysseus said that after a few days' travel he and his men came to another island. This one was home to a brutal, uncivilized people called Cyclopes. Each was a giant with a single eye in the center of his or her forehead. They "have no assemblies for the making of laws, nor any settled customs," Odysseus said. Rather, the crude giants

> *live in hollow caverns in the mountain heights, where each man is lawgiver to his children and his wives, and nobody cares a jot for his neighbors. [Also] the Cyclopes have nothing like our ships, [nor any] of that overseas traffic which ships have established between the nations.*

Name:
Poseidon

Roman name:
Neptune

Group:
Olympian

Family:
son of Cronus and Gaea, brother of Zeus

Responsibility:
the oceans

Symbols:
trident, horse, dolphin

Odysseus assumed the one-eyed creatures might prove troublesome and thought it best to avoid them. But the Greeks were out of food. So their leader chose 12 men and went ashore to search for supplies. Soon they came upon a large cave containing pens filled with sheep and goats. Odysseus ordered his men to grab some of the animals and head back to the ships. But before they could do so, the Cyclops who dwelled in the cave appeared and pushed an enormous rock across the entrance, trapping the Greeks inside.

Odysseus addressed the giant, whose name was Polyphemus: "We are Greeks on our way back from Troy, driven astray by contrary winds across a vast expanse of sea." He added: "You know the laws of hospitality. I beseech you, good sir, to remember your duty to the gods. For we throw ourselves on your mercy."

But the Cyclops would have none of it. "You must be a fool," he told Odysseus, "to preach to me of reverence for the gods. We Cyclopes care not a jot for Zeus . . . nor for the rest of the blessed gods."

At that point Polyphemus snatched up two of the Greeks and smashed their heads against the cave floor. As Odysseus told it:

> Their brains ran out on the ground and soaked the earth. Limb by limb, he tore them to pieces to make his meal, which he devoured like a mountain lion, never pausing till entrails and flesh, marrow and bones, were all consumed, while we could do nothing but weep and lift up our hands to Zeus in horror at the ghastly sight.

The next morning, Polyphemus killed two more men. Then he went out to tend to his flocks, making sure that the rock was securely in place in the doorway. On his return that evening, to Odysseus' horror, he ate two more Greeks. Then the Cyclops asked the leader of the remaining six men what his name was. Thinking quickly, Odysseus replied that his name was Nobody.

That night, after the giant had fallen asleep, the Greeks used their swords to sharpen a wooden pole. Then they heated its tip in a fire the Cyclops had lit earlier. Hefting the pole in a group effort, the men drove its red-hot tip right into the creature's huge eye. Polyphemus awakened with a start and shrieked at the top of his lungs. In Odysseus' words:

> He pulled the stake from his eye, streaming with blood. Then he hurled it away from him with frenzied hands and raised a great shout for the other Cyclopes who lived in neighboring caves along the windy heights. These, hearing his screams, came up [and] gathering outside the cave asked [him] "What on earth is wrong with you Polyphemus? Why must you disturb the peaceful night?" [Polyphemus answered] "O my friends, it's Nobody's treachery [that] is doing me to death!"

If nobody was assaulting him, they said, there was nothing to be done. So they went away.

The next morning the blinded Polyphemus pushed back the rock to let his livestock out to graze. He did not notice the Greeks clinging onto the undersides of the rams. They had escaped thanks to another of Odysseus' clever ideas. As they were boarding their ships, they heard the Cyclops crying out to his father for help. A chill went through the men when they heard the name the giant spoke. As it turned out, his father was none other than Poseidon, god of the seas. This did not bode well for Odysseus and his men, because now they had made a divine enemy.

Hurricane Winds and Cannibals

The deaths of six Greeks on the island of the Cyclopes proved only the beginning of Odysseus' troubles, he told the Phaeacian diners. More men were killed during the incident that followed. The ships arrived at the floating island of the deity of the winds, Aeolus.

Odysseus asked the god to help him and his men get back to Ithaca, and Aeolus agreed. He "presented me with a leather bag, made from the flayed skin of a full-grown ox," Odysseus recalled. Inside the bag

> he had imprisoned the boisterous energies of all the Winds. [This] pouch he stowed in the hold of my ship, securing it tightly with a burnished silver wire so as to prevent the slightest leakage. Then [he] called up a breeze from the west to blow my ships and their crews across the sea.

At first all went well. In less than a week, the excited men spied the green hills of Ithaca in the distance, at which point the exhausted Odysseus fell asleep. The moment he did so, some of his men were unable to resist finding out what was in the bag. One produced a knife and with it sliced open the leather container. Immediately, an unbelievably violent gust of wind burst forth, flattening several of the men like pancakes. Simultaneously, the hurricane-force storm sent the vessels careening all the way back to Aeolus' island. That god was so upset that he told the Greeks to go away and find their own way home.

The Greeks once more struck out for Ithaca. Six days passed, and they arrived at the island of a people called the Laestrygonians. Eleven of the 12 ships docked. Odysseus kept the 12th one anchored farther out to sea as a safety measure. This precaution proved more prudent than he'd imagined. Not only were the Laestrygonians much larger than the Greeks, they were also cannibals. Thousands of them ran down to the harbor. Screaming and drooling hideously, they boarded the ships and dragged the terrified sailors away to their doom. There was nothing that Odysseus and his crewmen on the 12th ship could do to help. Rowing like madmen, they barely escaped with their lives.

Laestrygonians were fearsome giant cannibals who attacked Odysseus and his men.

The Cannibals Attack

In Homer's account, Odysseus describes the attack by the vicious Laestrygonians:

In their thousands, [they were] more like giants than men. Standing at the top of the cliffs, they began pelting my fleet with lumps of rock such as a man could barely lift. And the din that now rose from the ships, where the groans of dying men could be heard above the splintering of timbers, was appalling. One by one they harpooned their prey like fish and carried them off to make their loathsome meal. But while this massacre was still going on in the depths of the harbor, I drew my sword [and] yelled to my crew to dash in with their oars if they wished to save their skins. With the fear of death upon them, they struck the water like one man, and with a sigh of relief, we shot out to sea. [My] ship was safe. But that was the end of all the rest.

Advice from the Dead

More weird and dangerous experiences followed. The last remaining vessel in Odysseus' fleet came to the island of Aeaea. It was the domain of a minor goddess and sorceress named Circe. She changed most of the Greeks into pigs. Only with the help of Hermes, patron god of travelers, was Odysseus able to force Circe to restore his men to their normal forms.

Before the men left the island, Circe offered them some advice. She told them that they would never reach their homes unless they sought out an old fortune-teller named Teiresias. But finding him would not be easy, she warned. That was because he was dead, and his shade (soul) roamed the Underworld.

Circe told Odysseus how to find an entrance to the dreary underground land of the dead. Following her directions, the men sailed for many days until they reached the shore of the Ocean, the remote river circling the world's outer edges. Then Odysseus dug a deep trench in the ground and prayed to the spirits of the dead. He promised them

> that directly when I got back to Ithaca, I shall sacrifice a [cow] in my palace [and] heap the pyre with treasures, and make Teiresias a separate offering of the finest jet-black sheep to be found in my flocks. When I had finished my prayers, [I] took the sheep and cut their throats over the trench so that the dark blood poured in. And now the souls of the dead . . . came swarming up [among them] fresh brides, unmarried youths, old men with life's long suffering behind them, [and] a great throng of warriors killed in battle.

Displeased with the Greek men, the sorceress Circe turned most of them into pigs.

Among the other dead souls who rose up to greet Odysseus was his own mother, Anticleia. She explained that assuming he was dead, she had died of grief. Another shade was that of Agamemnon, supreme commander of the Greeks who had sacked Troy. He said his wife had murdered him shortly after his return to Greece. Finally the spirit of old Teiresias appeared. He cautioned Odysseus that Poseidon was still very angry with him for blinding his son Polyphemus. Furthermore, the old man said, even after Odysseus made it back to Ithaca, his troubles would not be over. His beloved wife Penelope was plagued by a group of well-to-do suitors. Thinking that Odysseus had long been dead, each was demanding that she marry him.

The End of the Story

Hearing what his wife was going through made Odysseus more eager than ever to reach Ithaca. The problem was that the ship was still very far away from home. As near as the men could tell, they were on the far side of the island of Thrinacia (an ancient name for Sicily, off Italy's southwestern coast). In time they made it to the strait separating Thrinacia from Italy. There, to their surprise and horror, they encountered a frightening monster named Scylla. Towering over the ship, it grabbed six of Odysseus' men, dragged them away, and began devouring them. That allowed the rest to get away.

Minutes later the Greeks also had a narrow escape with a giant whirlpool called Charybdis. Odysseus later described what he had seen as they passed by it: "When she swallowed the salt water down, the whole interior of her vortex was exposed, the rocks re-echoed to her fearful roar, and the dark sands of the sea bottom came into view."

After their harrowing experiences in the strait, the men stopped to rest on Thrinacia's southeastern coast. There, some of them came upon some cattle and decided to slaughter and eat them. They did not realize that the animals belonged to Helios, god of the sun. Outraged by this act, Helios informed Zeus, who tossed a thunderbolt at the ship. The vessel was destroyed and all aboard except Odysseus were killed.

The disaster's lone survivor held onto a broken mast and drifted in the sea for nine days. Finally, he washed up on a beach in Ogygia, the island of the nymph Calypso. Convinced that she loved Odysseus, she forced him to remain with her for seven years. At the end of that period Athena prevailed upon Zeus to intervene. He ordered Calypso to free Odysseus, after which he made it to the land of the kindly Phaeacians. Thus did Odysseus come to the end of the story he told at the dinner party.

Home at Last

Delighted with Odysseus' tale of fantastic adventures, the king of the Phaeacians helped the storyteller make it back to Ithaca. Now 20 years older than when he'd left, Odysseus had no difficulty passing himself off as an old beggar. At first no one recognized him. The lone exception was his faithful dog Argus, who, even after all those years, instantly knew his master. The man and aged dog exchanged fond looks. Then Argus wagged his tail and closed his eyes for the last time. Odysseus surveyed the situation in his palace. Just as the shade of Teiresias had said, Penelope was beset by more than 100 suitors. They had recently demanded that she choose one of them as her husband and the new king of Ithaca.

Disgusted, the true king revealed himself to his son, Telemachus. After a tearful reunion, they hatched a plan to get rid of the suitors. Penelope had announced that she would stage an archery contest in the main banquet hall. She explained that Odysseus used to set up 12 ax heads in a row, with the holes in each lined up. Then he would shoot an arrow through all 12 ax heads without touching any of them. If one of the suitors could replicate that incredible shot using her husband's bow, she would agree to marry him.

The next day all the suitors arrived in the banquet hall, each ready to try his luck with the bow. None of them realized that Odysseus and Telemachus had locked them in. After several of the suitors had tried but failed to string Odysseus' great bow, he suddenly threw off his beggar's outfit. Seizing the bow, he strung it in an instant. Then he shot an arrow straight through the holes of the assembled axes.

Name:
Penelope

Roman name:
Penelope

Family:
wife of Odysseus,
mother of Telemachus

Known for:
being faithful throughout
Odysseus' 20-year
absence

Famous myth:
refusing the advances
of her many
persistent suitors

The startled suitors heard Odysseus tell them that their fates were sealed, words that made them panic. As they scurried in terror through the hall, the king, his son, and two loyal servants killed them one by one. They "hacked them down," Homer wrote. "Skulls cracked, the hideous groans of dying men were heard, and the whole floor ran with blood." A few minutes later, the shades of all the suitors were on their way to the House of Hades.

Penelope was the ever faithful wife of the king of Ithaca, the wandering Odysseus.

A Suitor Meets His End

As Odysseus slaughtered the suitors, one of them, Eurymachus, died a horrible death:

He drew his sharp and two-edged sword of bronze, and leapt at Odysseus with a terrible shout. But at the same moment the brave Odysseus let an arrow fly, which struck him by the nipple on his breast with such force that it pierced his liver. The sword dropped from his hand. Lurching across the table, he crumpled up and tumbled with it, hurling the food and wine-cup to the floor. In agony he dashed his forehead on the ground. His feet lashed out and overthrew the chair, and the fog of death descended on his eyes.

Odysseus not only won the archery contest but also gained revenge on his wife's suitors.

Soon after the fight in the banquet hall, Odysseus and Penelope were finally reunited. They returned to their bedchamber and, as Homer put it, "Glad indeed they were to lie once more together in the bed that had known them long ago." The two were so happy that they cried at the thought of ending their embrace. From afar, Athena heard their wish. The goddess prolonged the lovers' touching moment by delaying the coming of the dawn. She smiled, knowing that a soldier's long and difficult search for home was finally over.

Chapter 4
WHAT MAKES US WHO WE ARE?

A question often asked today is why the myths told in Homer's epics, the *Iliad* and *Odyssey*, and other Greek myths remain so popular. Why do new books about Greek mythology appear each year? Also, why do filmmakers continue to make movies based on myths? For instance, *Troy* (2004) was based on the *Iliad*, and *Clash of the Titans* (1981 and 2010) on the myth of Perseus and Medusa.

An important reason for the survival and ongoing popularity of these myths is that they provide a window into the past. The ancient Greeks invented or established many of Western society's cultural ideas and customs. In a very real sense, they are our great, great, great (and many more *greats)* grandparents. So interest in them and their civilization remains strong.

Brad Pitt (above) starred as Achilles in the 2004 film *Troy*.

One way to understand the lives and minds of that long-dead people is to look at their myths. The scholar Michael Grant pointed out:

The myths told by the Greeks [are] as important as history for our understanding of what [these] ancestors of our own civilization believed and thought and felt and expressed in writing and in visual art. For their mythology [was] interwoven [in complex ways with] the whole fabric of their public and private lives.

Irish novelist James Joyce based *Ulysses* on episodes from the *Odyssey*.

Every Greek, no matter how old, intimately knew the story of Achilles' slaying Hector before Troy's towering walls. The names and deeds of mythical characters were not merely mildly interesting facts from a distant past. Every Greek knew these names and deeds in the same way that modern Americans know their favorite TV, movie, and sports stars.

Moreover, the Greeks took everyday life lessons from the myths. For example, the punishments the gods meted out to Odysseus and his men taught ordinary Greeks the importance of revering and respecting these powerful deities. So examining the lessons and morals of those ancient stories reveals some of the social and ethical concepts the Greeks viewed as crucial.

Mythical Images Everywhere

Another important reason for learning about the characters and stories of the Greek myths is the degree to which they pervade our lives. References to them appear by the thousands in Western literature, films, and other media. One of the more famous literary examples is the 1831 poem "To Helen" by the famous master of horror, Edgar Allan Poe. Inspired by Helen of Troy, Poe wrote that her "classic face" had "brought me home" to "the glory that was Greece, and the grandeur that was Rome." In the 1920s the popular Irish novelist James Joyce was equally inspired by Homer. Joyce's *Ulysses*, based on the *Odyssey*, became one of the most beloved novels of modern times.

Famous for his tales of mystery, Edgar Allan Poe was inspired to write about Helen of Troy.

Pop culture images from the Greek myths abound.
Mobil Oil Company used a bright red figure of the
mythical flying horse Pegasus as its logo. A football
team, the Tennessee Titans, took its name from the first
race of Greek gods. Quite a few popular products also have the
names of mythical characters. Some examples are Ajax Cleanser
(named for the giant warrior in the *Iliad*); Midas Muffler (named
for the king whose touch turned objects into gold); and Nike
shoes (named for the Greek goddess of victory). The U.S. missions
to the moon in the 1960s and 1970s were named for the Greek
god of prophecy, Apollo. Several characters in the popular TV
show *Battlestar Galactica* are named after Greek gods and heroes.
And dozens of films, such as *Percy Jackson and the Olympians: The
Lightning Thief*, and video games, such as those in the *God of War*
series, feature mythical characters.

These are only a few examples of modern mythological
references. Listing all of them would fill a book hundreds of
pages long. Because the classic characters and stories surround
us, they cannot be ignored. As it was with our cultural ancestors,
the Greeks, the legends are part of what makes us who we are.
For that reason, Michael Grant said, the rediscovery of the Greek
myths "can be claimed as the most significant of all the impacts
that the [ancient Greek] world has made upon modern thought."

KEY FIGHTERS IN THE EPIC BATTLES

The Greeks

Achilles
Agamemnon
Ajax
Menelaus
Nestor
Odysseus
Patroclus
Peleus
The Myrmidons
(group of soldiers
from Phthia)

Gods on the Greeks' side
Athena • Hephaestus
Hera • Poseidon

Gods on the Trojans' side
Aphrodite • Apollo
Ares • Artemis

The Trojans

Men
Aeneas
Chryses
Hector
Paris
Priam

Women
Briseis
Chryseis
Hecuba
Helen

ADDITIONAL RESOURCES

Further Reading

Alexander, Caroline. *The War that Killed Achilles: The True Story of Homer's Iliad and the Trojan War*. New York: Viking, 2009.

Daly, Kathleen N. *Greek and Roman Mythology A to Z*. New York: Chelsea House, 2009.

Green, Roger L. *Tales of the Greek Heroes*. London: Puffin, 2009.

Hamby, Zachary. *Mythology for Teens: Classic Myths for Today's World*. Austin, Texas: Prufrock Press, 2009.

Nardo, Don. *Greek Mythology*. San Diego: KidHaven Press, 2002.

Sutcliff, Rosemary. *Black Ships Before Troy: The Story of the Iliad*. New York: Laurel Leaf, 2005.

Sutcliff, Rosemary. *The Wanderings of Odysseus*. New York: Laurel Leaf, 2005.

Internet Sites

Use FactHound to find Internet sites related to this book. All of the sites on FactHound have been researched by our staff.

Here's all you do:
Visit *www.facthound.com*
Type in this code:
9780756544829

GLOSSARY

Age of Heroes the period of the distant past in which the classical Greeks believed the stories told in their myths took place. Modern scholars call that era Greece's late Bronze Age and date it from about 1500 BC to 1150 BC.

alliance a union or bond

architectural related to designing and constructing buildings

armada a large fleet of ships

bard a storyteller

classical Greeks modern scholars date Greece's Classical Age to about 500 BC to 323 BC. More generally, the inhabitants of Greece between about 800 BC and 300 BC.

concept a general idea

culture all the beliefs, ideas, and values of a society

discord a lack of harmony, disagreement

entrails intestines or internal organs

epic a long poem, usually describing heroic acts

forge a smithy, or a place where metals are worked, by heating and hammering

hospitality kindness, welcoming attitude toward guests

House of Hades the Underworld, the dark realm of the dead overseen by the god Hades

immortality a state of living forever

intoxicating having the power to make someone tipsy or drunk

nymph a minor nature goddess

Olympians the group of gods led by Zeus and thought to live on top of Mount Olympus, Greece's highest mountain

Peloponnesus the large peninsula making up the southern third of the Greek mainland

prophecy the art or process of foretelling the future; or a specific prediction

pyre a funeral fire for burning the body

quiver a container for arrows worn on the body

reverence deep, often religious, respect

sacrilege words or deed that insults a god or religious beliefs

scribe in premodern times, a literate person hired to write letters or keep records

shade a soul or spirit of a dead person

spoils valuables, often seized in a war

suitor a man who tries to court or woo a woman

Western European-based

SOURCE NOTES

Chapter 1
The Dawn of Western Literature
Page 7, line 17: Michael Grant. *The Rise of the Greeks*.
New York: Macmillan, 1987, p. 147.
Page 8, line 9: Walter F. Otto. *The Homeric Gods*. Trans.
Moses Hades. New York: Random House, 1954, p. 16.
Page 9, line 9: Ernle Bradford. *Ulysses Found*. New York:
Harcourt, Brace and World, 1963, p. viii.

Chapter 2
The *Iliad:* A Warrior Refuses to Fight
Page 17, line 16: Homer. *Iliad*. Trans. E.V. Rieu. Baltimore:
Penguin, 1989, p. 24.
Page 18, line 20: Ibid, p. 32.
Page 18, line 23: Ibid, p. 33.
Page 19, line 3: Ibid, p. 36.
Page 21, line 8: Ibid, p. 73.
Page 21, line 12: Ibid, p. 74.
Page 22, lines 4, 9 : Ibid, p. 258.
Page 23, line 5: Ibid, pp. 267–268.
Page 23, line 15: Ibid, p. 278.
Page 23, sidebar: Ibid, p. 288.
Page 24, lines 7, 11: Ibid, p. 293.
Page 26, sidebar: Ibid, pp. 367–368.
Page 27, line 6: Ibid, p. 405.
Page 27, lines 15, 18: Ibid, pp. 405–406.

Chapter 3
The *Odyssey:* A Soldier Searches for Home
Page 37, line 6: Homer. *Odyssey*. Trans. E.V.Rieu.
Baltimore: Penguin, 1987, pp. 142–143.
Page 37, line 15: Ibid, p. 142.
Page 38, line 10: Ibid, p. 146.
Page 39, line 3: Ibid, p. 147.
Page 39, line 19: Ibid, p. 150.
Page 41, line 2: Ibid, p. 155.
Page 43, sidebar: Ibid, pp. 158–159.
Page 44, line 18: Ibid, pp. 171–172.
Page 47, line 3: Ibid, p. 195.
Page 49, line 6: Ibid, p. 336.
Page 50, sidebar: Ibid, p.330.
Page 51, line 6: Ibid, p. 348.

Chapter 4
What Makes Us Who We Are?
Page 53, line 3: Michael Grant. *Myths of the Greeks
and Romans*. New York: Plume, 1995, p. xvii.
Page 55, line 22: Edgar Allan Poe. *Complete Stories
and Poems of Edgar Allan Poe*. New York: Doubleday,
1984, p. 742.
page 57, line 7: *Myths of the Greeks and Romans*, p. xix.

SELECT BIBLIOGRAPHY

Ancient Sources

Hendricks, Rhoda A., ed. and trans., *Classical Gods and Heroes: Myths as Told by the Ancient Authors*. New York: Morrow Quill, 1974.

Homer. *Iliad*. Trans. E.V. Rieu. Baltimore: Penguin, 1989.

Homer. *Odyssey*. Trans. E.V. Rieu. Baltimore: Penguin, 1987.

Knox, Bernard M.W., ed., *The Norton Book of Classical Literature*. New York: W.W. Norton, 1993.

Modern Sources

Atchity, Kenneth, et al. *Critical Essays on Homer*. Boston: G.K. Hall, 1987.

Bellingham, David. *An Introduction to Greek Mythology*. Secaucus, N.J.: Chartwell Books, 2002.

Bowra, C.M. *Homer*. New York: Charles Scribner's Sons, 1972.

Fitton, J. Lesley. *The Discovery of the Greek Bronze Age*. Cambridge, Mass.: Harvard University Press, 2001.

Flacelière, Robert. *A Literary History of Greece*. Trans. Douglas Garman. Chicago: Aldine Publishing, 1968.

Grant, Michael. *A Guide to the Ancient World*. New York: Barnes and Noble, 1986.

Grant, Michael. *Myths of the Greeks and Romans*. New York: Plume, 1995.

Grant, Michael. *The Rise of the Greeks*. New York: Macmillan, 1987.

Grant, Michael, and John Hazel. *Who's Who in Classical Mythology*. London: Routledge, 2002.

Griffin, Jasper. *Homer on Life and Death*. Oxford, England: Clarendon Press, 1980.

Hamilton, Edith. *Mythology*. New York: Grand Central, 1999.

Hanson, Victor D., and John Heath. *Who Killed Homer? The Demise of Classical Education and the Recovery of Greek Wisdom*. New York: Free Press, 1998.

Kirk, G.S. *Homer and the Oral Tradition*. Cambridge, England: Cambridge University Press, 1976.

Morford, Mark P.O., and Robert J. Lenardon. *Classical Mythology*. New York: Oxford University Press, 2010.

Nardo, Don. *Greenhaven Encyclopedia of Greek and Roman Mythology*. San Diego: Greenhaven Press, 2002.

Rouse, W.H.D. *Gods, Heroes and Men of Ancient Greece*. New York: New American Library, 2001.

Sinclair, T.A. *A History of Classical Greek Literature, from Homer to Aristotle*. New York: Haskell House, 1973.

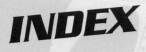

INDEX

About the author
Noted historian Don Nardo specializes in the ancient world and has published numerous books about Greek, Roman, Mesopotamian, and Egyptian mythology. He lives with his wife, Christine, in Massachusetts.